CONTENTS

FOREWORD

EVERYBODY loves to see a good game, well played; and everybody, who is anybody, loves a good player; and what the best in everybody naturally loves is pretty sure to be right. So if you, whoever you are, who read this, do not agree with what it says, you needn't have much doubt about it that you are wrong.

Of course, every one cannot play as well as every other person in every place in the game. One fellow can excel, say at football, and another at baseball, and another at scholarship; while some are physically unfitted to outclass their fellows at any of these

things. But that is no excuse whatever why they should not love every
good game and every good player.
To appreciate and encourage the
players is perhaps your part of the
game. Do not think that a good
"rooter" has no value.

Every one can excel in the greatest
of all games — the game of life. God
will give you exactly what you need
to win out in your particular place.

If you who are reading this do not
possess riches, or physical strength,
or genius, do not be discouraged.
Remember that riches of themselves
cannot add to your life anything
which is of real importance. Physical strength only belongs to any one
for a few years; and it has not been
the brilliantly clever, but the hard
workers who have given the world

most. That is, it is they who have
really won the greatest prize. For
success is measured, not by what we
have, but by what we do with what
we have. " 'Tis dogged as does it."
" Blessed be drudgery."

The second thing I want to say is
that no one, at heart, has any use
for the excuse maker. Even if you
know you cannot win, the world will
never forgive you for not trying. It
rightly despises the " quitter," but it
loves the fellow who says, " I know
I'm not much good, but I'll play the
game. I may not be able to get on
the gridiron, but I'll be there on my
place on the stand, and encourage
the others." The bigger the odds
against you, and the greater the sacrifice you have to make, the more
every one will love you, and the bet-

ter you will become fitted for accomplishment. Who cares for the winner of a "walkover"? The man who is worth while does not care about it himself. Anyhow, there is no such thing as a "walkover" in the greatest game of all. There is only one way to attain the best of all prizes, that is to fight for it, and win it for yourself.

This little book is only the story of a Doctor in the wilds. His name and his identity do not matter. They will soon be forgotten anyhow. It was only a nameless fisher-lad whose life was at issue. The world does not care whether it was prolonged or not. What at first to us appear the big things, are really, often enough, only the little things.

If there is any lesson, it is only of

importance in showing that the playing of the game well is in itself the prize of life, and that now is the time, and exactly where you are is the place, for each man to be playing it.

Our own approval, and the world's approval, and God's approval can only be gained by struggle. They can never be purchased. Life is not a gamble. The crown of life can only go, and will always go, to those who have a right to say "I have fought a good fight." Captain Oates won it when he went out to meet death, consciously, in order that he might try and save his companions. All the ages concede that Christ won it, though it was on a cross. Nathan Hale, scholar and athlete, emphasized this when, as he gladly gave up his young life for his country, he

FOREWORD

said, "My only regret is that I have but one life to offer."

WILFRED T. GRENFELL, M.D.

November 5, 1913.

BIOGRAPHICAL SKETCH

" MOST NOBLE VICE-CHANCELLOR,
      AND YOU, EMINENT PROCTORS:

" A citizen of Britain is before you, once a student in this University, now better known to the people of the New World than to our own. This is the man who fifteen years ago went to the coast of Labrador, to succor with medical aid the solitary fishermen of the northern sea ; in executing which service he despised the perils of the ocean, which are there most terrible, in order to bring comfort and light to the wretched and sorrowing. Thus, up to the mea-sure of human ability, he seems to fol-

[xi]

low, if it is right to say it of any one, in the footsteps of Christ Himself, as a truly Christian man. Rightly then we praise him by whose praise not he alone, but our University also is honored. I present to you Wilfred Thomason Grenfell, that he may be admitted to the degree of Doctor in Medicine, HONORIS CAUSA."

Thus may be rendered the Latin address when, in May, 1907, for the first time in its history, the University of Oxford conferred the honorary degree in medicine. With these fitting words was presented a man whose simple faith has been the motive power of his works, to whom pain and weariness of flesh have called no stay since there was discouragement never, to whom personal danger has counted as nothing since fear

BIOGRAPHICAL SKETCH

is incomprehensible. "As the Lord wills, whether for wreck or service, I am about His business." On November 9th of the preceding year, the King of England gave one of his "Birthday Honors" to the same man, making him a Companion of Saint Michael and Saint George (C.M.G.).

Wilfred Thomason Grenfell, second son of the Reverend Algernon Sydney Grenfell and Jane Georgiana Hutchinson, was born on February 28, 1865, at Mostyn House School, Parkgate, by Chester, England, of an ancestry which laid a firm foundation for his career and in surroundings which fitted him for it. On both sides of his inheritance have been exhibited the courage, patience, persistence, and fighting and teaching qualities which are exemplified in his own abilities to command, to administer, and to uplift.

On his father's side were the Grenvilles, who made good account of themselves in such cause as they approved, among them Basil Grenville, commander of the Royalist Cornish Army, killed at Lansdown in 1643 in defence of King Charles.

> " Four wheels to Charles's wain :
>   Grenville, Trevanion, Slanning, Godolphin
>   slain."

There was also Sir Richard Grenville, immortalized by Tennyson in " The Revenge," and John Pascoe Grenville, the right-hand man of Admiral Cochrane, who boarded the Spanish admiral's ship, the Esmeralda, on the port side, while Cochrane came up on the starboard, when together they made short work of the capture. Nor has the strain died out, as is demonstrated in the present generation by many of Dr. Grenfell's cousins, among them General Francis Wallace Grenfell, Lord Kilvey, and by Dr. Grenfell himself on the Labrador in the fight against disease and disaster and distress along a stormy and uncharted coast.

On his mother's side, four of her brothers were generals or colonels in the trying times of service in India. The eldest fought with distinction throughout the Indian Mutiny and in the defence of Lucknow, and another commanded the crack cavalry regiment, the "Guides," at Peshawar, and fell fighting in one of the turbulent North of India wars.

Of teachers, there was Dr. Grenfell's paternal grandfather, the Rev-

erend Algernon Grenfell, the second
of three brothers, house master at
Rugby under Arnold, and a fine
classical scholar, whose elder and
younger brothers each felt the an-
cestral call of the sea and became
admirals, with brave records of daring and success.

Dr. Grenfell's father, after a bril-
liant career at Rugby School and at
Balliol College, Oxford, became as-
sistant master at Repton, and later,
when he married, head master of
Mostyn House School, a position
which he resigned in 1882 to become
Chaplain of the London Hospital.
"He was a man of much learning,
with a keen interest in science, a re-
markable eloquence, and a fervent
evangelistic faith."

Mostyn House School still stands,

enlarged and modernized, in the charge of Dr. Grenfell's elder brother, and in it his mother is still the real head and controlling genius.

Parkgate, at one time a seaport of renown, when Liverpool was still unimportant, and later a seaside health resort to which came the fashion and beauty of England, had fallen, through the silting of the estuary and the broadening of the "Sands of Dee," to the level of a hamlet in the time of Dr. Grenfell's boyhood. The broad stretch of seaward trending sand, with its interlacing rivulets of fresh and brackish water, made a tempting though treacherous playground, alluring alike in the varied forms of life it harbored and in the adventure which whetted exploration. Thither came Charles Kingsley,

Canon of Chester, who married a Grenfell, and who coupled his verse with scientific study and made geological excursions to the river's mouth with the then Master of Mostyn House School. In these excursions the youthful Wilfred was a participant, and therein he learned some of his first lessons in that accuracy of observation essential to his later life work.

Here in this trained, but untrammeled, boyhood, with an inherited incentive to labor and an educated thirst for knowledge, away from the thrall of crowded communities, close to the wild places of nature, with the sea always beckoning and a rocking boat as familiar as the land, it is small wonder that there grew the fashioning of the purpose of a man, dimly at first, conceived in a home in which all, both of tradition and of teaching, bred faith, reverence, and the sense of thanksgiving in usefulness.

From the school-days at Parkgate came the step to Marlborough College, where three years were marked by earnest study, both in books and in play, for the one gained a scholarship and the other an enduring interest in Rugby football. Matriculating later at the University of London, Grenfell entered the London Hospital, and there laid not only the foundation of his medical education, but that of his friendship with Sir Frederick Treves, renowned surgeon and daring sailor and master mariner as well. With plenty of work to the fore, as a hospital interne, the ruling

spirit still asserted itself, and the
young doctor became an inspiration
among the waifs of the teeming city;
he was one of the founders of the
great Lads' Brigades which have done
much good, and fostered more, in
the example that they have set for
allied activities. Nor were the needs
of his own bodily machine neglected;
football, rowing, and the tennis court
kept him in condition, and his ath-
letics served to strengthen his appeals
to the London boys whom he enrolled
in the brigades. He founded the inter-
hospital rowing club at Putney and
rowed in the first inter-hospital race;
he played on the Varsity football
team, and won the ''throwing the
hammer'' at the sports.

A couple of terms at Queen's College, Oxford, followed the London

experience, but here the conditions were too easy and luxurious for one who, by both inheritance and training, had within him the incentive to the strenuous life. Need called, misery appealed, the message of life, of hope, and of salvation awaited, and the young doctor turned from Oxford to the medical mission work in which his record stands among the foremost for its effectiveness and for the spirituality of its purpose.

Seeking some way in which he could satisfy his medical aspirations, as well as his desire for adventure and for definite Christian work, he appealed to Sir Frederick Treves, a member of the Council of the Royal National Mission to Deep Sea Fishermen, who suggested his joining the staff of the mission and establishing a medical mission to the fishermen of the North Sea. The conditions of the life were onerous, the existing traffic in spirituous liquors and in all other demoralizing influences had to be fought step by step, prejudice and evil habit had to be overcome and to be replaced by better knowledge and better desire, there was room for both fighting and teaching, and the medical mission won its way. "When you set out to commend your gospel to men who don't want it, there's only one way to go about it — to do something for them that they'll be sure to understand. The message of love that was 'made flesh and dwelt amongst men' must be reincarnate in our lives if it is to be received to-day." Thus came about the outfitting of the Albert hospital ship to carry the message and the help, by cruising among the fleets on the fishing-grounds, and the organization of the Deep Sea Mission; when this work was done, "when the fight had gone out of it," Dr. Grenfell looked for another field, for yet another need, and found it on that barren and inhospitable coast the Labrador, whose only harvest field is the sea.

Six hundred miles of almost barren rock with outlying uncharted ledges — worn smooth by ice, else still more vessels would have found wreckage there; a scant, constant population of hardy fishermen and their families, pious and God-fearing, most of them, but largely at the mercy of the local traders, who took their pay in fish for the bare necessities of living, with a large account always on the trader's side; with such medical aid and ministration as came only occasionally, by the infrequent mail boat, and not at all in the long winter months when the coast was firm beset with ice — to such a place came Dr. Grenfell in 1892 to cast in his lot with its inhabitants, to live there so long as he should, to die there were it God's will.

As it stands to-day, the Mission to Deep Sea Fishermen, which Dr. Grenfell represents, administers, and animates on the Labrador coast, not only brings hope, new courage, and spiritual comfort to an isolated people in a desolate land, but cares for the sick and injured, in its four hospitals and dispensary, provides

house visitation by means of dog-
sledge journeys covering hundreds
of miles in a year, teaches whole-
some and righteous living, conducts
coöperative stores, provides for or-
phans and for families bereft of the
bread-winners by accidents of the
sea, encourages thrift, and administers justice, and adds to the wage-
earning capacity and therefore food-
obtaining power by operating a saw-
mill, a schooner-building yard, and
other productive industries.

To accomplish this, to make of the
scattered settlements a united and
independent people, to safeguard
their future by such measures as the
establishment of a Seamen's Insti-
tute at St. John's, Newfoundland,
and the insurance of communication
with the outside world, and to raise,

BIOGRAPHICAL SKETCH

by personal solicitation, the money
needed for these enterprises, re-
quires an unusual personality. Faith,
courage, insight, foresight, the power to win, and the ability to command — all of these and more of like
qualities are embodied and portrayed
in Dr. Grenfell.

CLARENCE JOHN BLAKE

ADRIFT ON AN ICE-PAN

IT was Easter Sunday at St. Anthony in the year 1908, but with us in northern Newfoundland still winter. Everything was covered with snow and ice. I was walking back after morning service, when a boy came running over from the hospital with the news that a large team of dogs had come from sixty miles to the southward, to get a doctor on a very urgent case. It was that of a young man on whom we had operated about a fortnight before for an acute bone disease in the thigh. The people had allowed the wound to close, the poisoned matter had accumulated, and we thought we should have to remove the leg. There was obviously, therefore, no time to be lost. So, having packed up the necessary instruments, dressings, and drugs, and having fitted out the dog-sleigh with my best dogs, I started at once, the messengers following me with their team.

My team was an especially good one. On many a long journey they had stood by me and pulled me out of difficulties by their sagacity and endurance. To a lover of his dogs, as every Christian man must be, each one had become almost as precious as a child to its mother. They were beautiful beasts: "Brin," the cleverest leader on the coast; "Doc," a large, gentle beast, the backbone of the team for power; "Spy," a wiry, powerful black and white dog;

"Moody," a lop-eared black-and-tan, in his third season, a plodder that never looked behind him; "Watch," the youngster of the team, long-legged and speedy, with great liquid eyes and a Gordon-setter coat; "Sue," a large, dark Eskimo, the image of a great black wolf, with her sharp-pointed and perpendicular ears, for she "harked back" to her wild ancestry; "Jerry," a large roan-colored slut, the quickest of all my dogs on her feet, and so affectionate that her overtures of joy had often sent me sprawling on my back; "Jack," a jet-black, gentle-natured dog, more like a retriever, that always ran next the sledge, and never looked back but everlastingly pulled straight ahead, running always with his nose to the ground.

ADRIFT ON AN ICE-PAN

It was late in April, when there is
always the risk of getting wet through
the ice, so that I was carefully pre-
pared with spare outfit, which in-
cluded a change of garments, snow-
shoes, rifle, compass, axe, and oilskin
overclothes. The messengers were
anxious that their team should travel
back with mine, for they were slow
at best and needed a lead. My dogs,
however, being a powerful team,
could not be held back, and though
I managed to wait twice for their
sleigh, I had reached a village about
twenty miles on the journey before
nightfall, and had fed the dogs, and
was gathering a few people for prayers when they caught me up.

During the night the wind shifted
to the northeast, which brought in
fog and rain, softened the snow, and

made travelling very bad, besides heaving a heavy sea into the bay. Our drive next morning would be somewhat over forty miles, the first ten miles on an arm of the sea, on salt-water ice.

In order not to be separated too long from my friends, I sent them ahead two hours before me, appointing a rendezvous in a log tilt that we have built in the woods as a halfway house. There is no one living on all that long coast-line, and to provide against accidents — which have happened more than once — we built this hut to keep dry clothing, food, and drugs in.

The first rain of the year was falling when I started, and I was obliged to keep on what we call the "ballicaters," or ice barricades, much farther

[5]

up the bay than I had expected. The sea of the night before had smashed the ponderous covering of ice right to the landwash. There were great gaping chasms between the enormous blocks, which we call pans, and half a mile out it was all clear water.

An island three miles out had preserved a bridge of ice, however, and by crossing a few cracks I managed to reach it. From the island it was four miles across to a rocky promontory — a course that would be several miles shorter than going round the shore. Here as far as the eye could reach the ice seemed good, though it was very rough. Obviously, it had been smashed up by the sea and then packed in again by the strong wind from the northeast, and I thought it had frozen together solid.

All went well till I was about a quarter of a mile from the landing-point. Then the wind suddenly fell, and I noticed that I was travelling over loose " sish," which was like porridge and probably many feet deep. By stabbing down, I could drive my whip-handle through the thin coating of young ice that was floating on it. The sish ice consists of the tiny fragments where the large pans have been pounding together on the heaving sea, like the stones of Freya's grinding mill.

So quickly did the wind now come off shore, and so quickly did the packed "slob," relieved of the wind pressure, "run abroad," that already I could not see one pan larger than ten feet square; moreover, the ice was loosening so rapidly that I saw

that retreat was absolutely impossible. Neither was there any way to get
off the little pan I was surveying
from.

There was not a moment to lose.
I tore off my oilskins, threw myself
on my hands and knees by the side
of the komatik to give a larger base
to hold, and shouted to my team to
go ahead for the shore. Before we
had gone twenty yards, the dogs got
frightened, hesitated for a moment,
and the komatik instantly sank into
the slob. It was necessary then for
the dogs to pull much harder, so that
they now began to sink in also.

Earlier in the season the father of
the very boy I was going to operate
on had been drowned in this same
way, his dogs tangling their traces
around him in the slob. This flashed

into my mind, and I managed to loosen my sheath-knife, scramble forward, find the traces in the water, and cut them, holding on to the leader's trace wound round my wrist.

Being in the water I could see no piece of ice that would bear anything up. But there was as it happened a piece of snow, frozen together like a large snowball, about twenty-five yards away, near where my leading dog, "Brin," was wallowing in the slob. Upon this he very shortly climbed, his long trace of ten fathoms almost reaching there before he went into the water.

This dog has weird black markings on his face, giving him the appearance of wearing a perpetual grin. After climbing out on the snow, as if it were the most natural position in the world, he deliberately shook the ice and water from his long coat, and then turned round to look for me. As he sat perched up there out of the water, he seemed to be grinning with satisfaction. The other dogs were hopelessly bogged. Indeed, we were like flies in treacle.

Gradually, I hauled myself along the line that was still tied to my wrist, till without any warning the dog turned round and slipped out of his harness, and then once more turned his grinning face to where I was struggling.

It was impossible to make any progress through the sish ice by swimming, so I lay there and thought all would soon be over, only wondering if any one would ever know how it happened. There was no particu-

lar horror attached to it, and in fact I
began to feel drowsy, as if I could easily go to sleep, when suddenly I saw
the trace of another big dog that
had himself gone through before he
reached the pan, and though he was
close to it was quite unable to force
his way out. Along this I hauled myself, using him as a bow anchor, but
much bothered by the other dogs as
I passed them, one of which got
on my shoulder, pushing me farther
down into the ice. There was only a
yard or so more when I had passed
my living anchor, and soon I lay
with my dogs around me on the little
piece of slob ice. I had to help them
on to it, working them through the
lane that I had made.

The piece of ice we were on was
so small, it was obvious we must soon

all be drowned, if we remained upon
it as it drifted seaward into more open
water. If we were to save our lives,
no time was to be lost. When I stood
up, I could see about twenty yards
away a larger pan floating amidst the
sish, like a great flat raft, and if we
could get on to it we should post-
pone at least for a time the death that
already seemed almost inevitable.
It was impossible to reach it without
a life line, as I had already learned to
my cost, and the next problem was
how to get one there. Marvellous to
relate, when I had first fallen through,
after I had cut the dogs adrift without
any hope left of saving myself, I had
not let my knife sink, but had fastened
it by two half hitches to the back
of one of the dogs. To my great joy
there it was still, and shortly I was

at work cutting all the sealskin traces
still hanging from the dogs' harnesses, and splicing them together
into one long line. These I divided
and fastened to the backs of my two
leaders, tying the near ends round
my two wrists. I then pointed out to
"Brin" the pan I wanted to reach
and tried my best to make them go
ahead, giving them the full length
of my lines from two coils. My long
sealskin moccasins, reaching to my
thigh, were full of ice and water.
These I took off and tied separately
on the dogs' backs. My coat, hat,
gloves, and overalls I had already
lost. At first, nothing would induce
the two dogs to move, and though I
threw them off the pan two or three
times, they struggled back upon it,
which perhaps was only natural,

because as soon as they fell through they could see nowhere else to make for. To me, however, this seemed to spell "the end." Fortunately, I had with me a small black spaniel, almost a featherweight, with large furry paws, called "Jack," who acts as my mascot and incidentally as my retriever. This at once flashed into my mind, and I felt I had still one more chance for life. So I spoke to him and showed him the direction, and then threw a piece of ice toward the desired goal. Without a moment's hesitation he made a dash for it, and to my great joy got there safely, the tough scale of sea ice carrying his weight bravely. At once I shouted to him to "lie down," and this, too, he immediately did, looking like a little black fuzz ball on the white setting.

My leaders could now see him seated there on the new piece of floe, and when once more I threw them off they understood what I wanted, and fought their way to where they saw the spaniel, carrying with them the line that gave me the one chance for my life. The other dogs followed them, and after painful struggling, all got out again except one. Taking all the run that I could get on my little pan, I made a dive, slithering with the impetus along the surface till once more I sank through. After a long fight, however, I was able to haul myself by the long traces on to this new pan, having taken care beforehand to tie the harnesses to which I was holding under the dogs' bellies, so that they could not slip them off. But alas! the pan I was now on was not large enough to bear us and was already beginning to sink, so this process had to be repeated immediately.

I now realized that, though we had been working toward the shore, we had been losing ground all the time, for the off-shore wind had already driven us a hundred yards farther out. But the widening gap kept full of the pounded ice, through which no man could possibly go.

I had decided I would rather stake my chances on a long swim even than perish by inches on the floe, as there was no likelihood whatever of being seen and rescued. But, keenly though I watched, not a streak even of clear water appeared, the interminable sish rising from below and filling every gap as it appeared. We were now resting on a piece of ice about ten by twelve feet, which, as I found when I came to examine it, was not ice at all, but simply snow-covered slob frozen into a mass, and I feared it would very soon break up in the general turmoil of the heavy sea, which was increasing as the ice drove off shore before the wind.

At first we drifted in the direction of a rocky point on which a heavy surf was breaking. Here I thought once again to swim ashore. But suddenly we struck a rock. A large piece broke off the already small pan, and what was left swung round in the backwash, and started right out to sea.

There was nothing for it now but to hope for a rescue. Alas! there was little possibility of being seen. As I

[17]

have already mentioned, no one lives around this big bay. My only hope was that the other komatik, knowing I was alone and had failed to keep my tryst, would perhaps come back to look for me. This, however, as it proved, they did not do.

The westerly wind was rising all the time, our coldest wind at this time of the year, coming as it does over the Gulf ice. It was tantalizing, as I stood with next to nothing on, the wind going through me and every stitch soaked in ice-water, to see my well-stocked komatik some fifty yards away. It was still above water, with food, hot tea in a thermos bottle, dry clothing, matches, wood, and everything on it for making a fire to attract attention.

It is easy to see a dark object on

the ice in the daytime, for the gorgeous whiteness shows off the least thing. But the tops of bushes and large pieces of kelp have often deceived those looking out. Moreover, within our memory no man has been thus adrift on the bay ice. The chances were about one in a thousand that I should be seen at all, and if I were seen, I should probably be mistaken for some piece of refuse.

To keep from freezing, I cut off my long moccasins down to the feet, strung out some line, split the legs, and made a kind of jacket, which protected my back from the wind down as far as the waist. I have this jacket still, and my friends assure me it would make a good Sunday garment.

I had not drifted more than half

a mile before I saw my poor komatik disappear through the ice, which was every minute loosening up into the small pans that it consisted of, and it seemed like a friend gone and one more tie with home and safety lost. To the northward, about a mile distant, lay the mainland along which I had passed so merrily in the morning—only, it seemed, a few moments before.

By mid-day I had passed the island to which I had crossed on the ice bridge. I could see that the bridge was gone now. If I could reach the island I should only be marooned and destined to die of starvation. But there was little chance of that, for I was rapidly driving into the ever widening bay.

It was scarcely safe to move on

my small ice raft, for fear of breaking it. Yet I saw I must have the
skins of some of my dogs — of which
I had eight on the pan — if I was to
live the night out. There was now
some three to five miles between me
and the north side of the bay. There,
immense pans of Arctic ice, surging
to and fro on the heavy ground seas,
were thundering into the cliffs like
medieval battering-rams. It was evi-
dent that, even if seen, I could hope
for no help from that quarter before
night. No boat could live through the
surf.

Unwinding the sealskin traces from
my waist, round which I had wound
them to keep the dogs from eating
them, I made a slip-knot, passed it
over the first dog's head, tied it round
my foot close to his neck, threw him

on his back, and stabbed him in the heart. Poor beast! I loved him like a friend — a beautiful dog — but we could not all hope to live. In fact, I had no hope any of us would, at that time, but it seemed better to die fighting.

In spite of my care the struggling dog bit me rather badly in the leg. I suppose my numb hands prevented my holding his throat as I could ordinarily do. Moreover, I must hold the knife in the wound to the end, as blood on the fur would freeze solid and make the skin useless. In this way I sacrificed two more large dogs, receiving only one more bite, though I fully expected that the pan I was on would break up in the struggle. The other dogs, who were licking their coats and trying to get dry, apparently took no notice of the fate of their comrades — but I was very careful to prevent the dying dogs crying out, for the noise of fighting would probably have been followed by the rest attacking the down dog, and that was too close to me to be pleasant. A short shrift seemed to me better than a long one, and I envied the dead dogs whose troubles were over so quickly. Indeed, I came to balance in my mind whether, if once I passed into the open sea, it would not be better by far to use my faithful knife on myself than to die by inches. There seemed no hardship in the thought. I seemed fully to sympathize with the Japanese view of hara-kiri.

Working, however, saved me from philosophizing. By the time I had skinned these dogs, and with my knife and some of the harness had strung the skins together, I was ten miles on my way, and it was getting dark.

Away to the northward I could see a single light in the little village where I had slept the night before, where I had received the kindly hospitality of the simple fishermen in whose comfortable homes I have spent many a night. I could not help but think of them sitting down to tea, with no idea that there was any one watching them, for I had told them not to expect me back for three days.

Meanwhile I had frayed out a small piece of rope into oakum, and mixed it with fat from the intestines of my dogs. Alas, my match-box, which was always chained to me, had leaked, and my matches were in pulp. Had I been able to make a light, it would have looked so unearthly out there on the sea that I felt sure they would see me. But that chance was now cut off. However, I kept the matches, hoping that I might dry them if I lived through the night. While working at the dogs, about every five minutes I would stand up and wave my hands toward the land. I had no flag, and I could not spare my shirt, for, wet as it was, it was better than nothing in that freezing wind, and, anyhow, it was already nearly dark.

Unfortunately, the coves in among the cliffs are so placed that only for a very narrow space can the people in any house see the sea. Indeed, most of them cannot see it at all, so that I could not in the least expect any one to see me, even supposing it had been daylight.

Not daring to take any snow from the surface of my pan to break the wind with, I piled up the carcasses of my dogs. With my skin rug I could now sit down without getting soaked. During these hours I had continually taken off all my clothes, wrung them out, swung them one by one in the wind, and put on first one and then the other inside, hoping that what heat there was in my body would thus serve to dry them. In this I had been fairly successful.

My feet gave me most trouble, for they immediately got wet again be-cause my thin moccasins were easily soaked through on the snow. I suddenly thought of the way in which the Lapps who tend our reindeer manage for dry socks. They carry grass with them, which they ravel up and pad into their shoes. Into this they put their feet, and then pack the rest with more grass, tying up the top with a binder. The ropes of the harness for our dogs are carefully sewed all over with two layers of flannel in order to make them soft against the dogs' sides. So, as soon as I could sit down, I started with my trusty knife to rip up the flannel. Though my fingers were more or less frozen, I was able also to ravel out the rope, put it into my shoes, and use my wet socks inside my knicker-bockers, where, though damp, they served to break the wind. Then, tying the narrow strips of flannel together, I bound up the top of the moccasins, Lapp–fashion, and carried the bandage on up over my knee, making a ragged though most excellent puttee.

As to the garments I wore, I had opened recently a box of football clothes I had not seen for twenty years. I had found my old Oxford University football running shorts and a pair of Richmond Football Club red, yellow, and black stockings, exactly as I wore them twenty years ago. These with a flannel shirt and sweater vest were now all I had left. Coat, hat, gloves, oilskins, everything else, were gone, and I stood there in that odd costume, exactly as I stood twenty years ago on a football field, reminding me of the little girl of a friend, who, when told she was

dying, asked to be dressed in her
Sunday frock to go to heaven in. My
costume, being very light, dried all
the quicker, until afternoon. Then
nothing would dry any more, everything freezing stiff. It had been an
ideal costume to struggle through
the slob ice. I really believe the con-
ventional garments missionaries are
supposed to affect would have been
fatal.

My occupation till what seemed
like midnight was unravelling rope,
and with this I padded out my knickers inside, and my shirt as well,
though it was a clumsy job, for I
could not see what I was doing. Now,
getting my largest dog, Doc, as big
as a wolf and weighing ninety-two
pounds, I made him lie down, so that
I could cuddle round him. I then

wrapped the three skins around me, arranging them so that I could lie on one edge, while the other came just over my shoulders and head.

My own breath collecting inside the newly flayed skin must have had a soporific effect, for I was soon fast asleep. One hand I had kept warm against the curled up dog, but the other, being gloveless, had frozen, and I suddenly awoke, shivering enough, I thought, to break my fragile pan. What I took at first to be the sun was just rising, but I soon found it was the moon, and then I knew it was about half-past twelve. The dog was having an excellent time. He hadn't been cuddled so warm all winter, and he resented my moving with low growls till he found it wasn't another dog.

The wind was steadily driving me now toward the open sea, and I could expect, short of a miracle, nothing but death out there. Somehow, one scarcely felt justified in praying for a miracle. But we have learned down here to pray for things we want, and, anyhow, just at that moment the miracle occurred. The wind fell off suddenly, and came with a light air from the southward, and then dropped stark calm. The ice was now "all abroad," which I was sorry for, for there was a big safe pan not twenty yards away from me. If I could have got on that, I might have killed my other dogs when the time came, and with their coats I could hope to hold out for two or three days more, and with the food and drink their bodies would offer

me need not at least die of hunger
or thirst. To tell the truth, they were
so big and strong I was half afraid to
tackle them with only a sheath-knife
on my small and unstable raft.

But it was now freezing hard. I
knew the calm water between us
would form into cakes, and I had
to recognize that the chance of getting near enough to escape on to it
was gone. If, on the other hand, the
whole bay froze solid again I had yet
another possible chance. For my pan
would hold together longer and I
should be opposite another village,
called Goose Cove, at daylight, and
might possibly be seen from there.
I knew that the komatiks there would
be starting at daybreak over the hills
for a parade of Orangemen about
twenty miles away. Possibly, there-

fore, I might be seen as they climbed the hills. So I lay down, and went to sleep again.

It seems impossible to say how long one sleeps, but I woke with a sudden thought in my mind that I must have a flag; but again I had no pole and no flag. However, I set to work in the dark to disarticulate the legs of my dead dogs, which were now frozen stiff, and which were all that offered a chance of carrying anything like a distress signal. Cold as it was, I determined to sacrifice my shirt for that purpose with the first streak of daylight.

It took a long time in the dark to get the legs off, and when I had patiently marled them together with old harness rope and the remains of the skin traces, it was the heaviest

and crookedest flag-pole it has ever
been my lot to see. I had had no food
from six o'clock the morning before,
when I had eaten porridge and bread
and butter. I had, however, a rub-
ber band which I had been wearing
instead of one of my garters, and I
chewed that for twenty-four hours.
It saved me from thirst and hunger,
oddly enough. It was not possible
to get a drink from my pan, for it
was far too salty. But anyhow that
thought did not distress me much,
for as from time to time I heard the
cracking and grinding of the newly
formed slob, it seemed that my devoted boat must inevitably soon go
to pieces.

At last the sun rose, and the time
came for the sacrifice of my shirt. So
I stripped, and, much to my surprise,

found it not half so cold as I had anticipated. I now re-formed my dog-skins with the raw side out, so that they made a kind of coat quite rivalling Joseph's. But, with the rising of the sun, the frost came out of the joints of my dogs' legs, and the friction caused by waving it made my flag-pole almost tie itself in knots. Still, I could raise it three or four feet above my head, which was very important.

Now, however, I found that instead of being as far out at sea as I had reckoned, I had drifted back in a northwesterly direction, and was off some cliffs known as Ireland Head. Near these there was a little village looking seaward, whence I should certainly have been seen. But, as I had myself, earlier in the winter, been night-bound at this place, I had learnt there was not a single soul living there at all this winter. The people had all, as usual, migrated to the winter houses up the bay, where they get together for schooling and social purposes.

I soon found it was impossible to keep waving so heavy a flag all the time, and yet I dared not sit down, for that might be the exact moment some one would be in a position to see me from the hills. The only thing in my mind was how long I could stand up and how long go on waving that pole at the cliffs. Once or twice I thought I saw men against their snowy faces, which, I judged, were about five and a half miles from me, but they were only trees. Once, also, I thought I saw a boat approaching.

A glittering object kept appearing and disappearing on the water, but it was only a small piece of ice sparkling in the sun as it rose on the surface. I think that the rocking of my cradle up and down on the waves had helped me to sleep, for I felt as well as ever I did in my life; and with the hope of a long sunny day, I felt sure I was good to last another twenty-four hours — if my boat would hold out and not rot under the sun's rays.

Each time I sat down to rest, my big dog "Doc" came and kissed my face and then walked to the edge of the ice-pan, returning again to where I was huddled up, as if to say, "Why don't you come along? Surely it is time to start." The other dogs also were now moving about very restlessly, occasionally trying to satisfy their hunger by gnawing at the dead bodies of their brothers.

I determined, at mid-day, to kill a big Eskimo dog and drink his blood, as I had read only a few days before in "Farthest North" of Dr. Nansen's doing — that is, if I survived the battle with him. I could not help feeling, even then, my ludicrous position, and I thought, if ever I got ashore again, I should have to laugh at myself standing hour after hour waving my shirt at those lofty cliffs, which seemed to assume a kind of sardonic grin, so that I could almost imagine they were laughing at me. At times I could not help thinking of the good breakfast that my colleagues were enjoying at the back of those same cliffs, and of the snug fire and the comfortable room which we call our study.

I can honestly say that from first to last not a single sensation of fear entered my mind, even when I was struggling in the slob ice. Somehow it did not seem unnatural; I had been through the ice half a dozen times before. For the most part I felt very sleepy, and the idea was then very strong in my mind that I should soon reach the solution of the mysteries that I had been preaching about for so many years.

Only the previous night (Easter Sunday) at prayers in the cottage, we had been discussing the fact that the soul was entirely separate from the body, that Christ's idea of the body as the temple in which the soul dwells is so amply borne out by modern science. We had talked of thoughts from that admirable book,

"Brain and Personality," by Dr. Thompson of New York, and also of the same subject in the light of a recent operation performed at the Johns Hopkins Hospital by Dr. Harvey Cushing. The doctor had removed from a man's brain two large cystic tumors without giving the man an anæsthetic, and the patient had kept up a running conversation with him all the while the doctor's fingers were working in his brain. It had seemed such a striking proof that ourselves and our bodies are two absolutely different things.

Our eternal life has always been with me a matter of faith. It seems to me one of those problems that must always be a mystery to knowledge. But my own faith in this matter had been so untroubled that it seemed now almost natural to be leaving through this portal of death from an ice-pan. In many ways, also, I could see how a death of this kind might be of value to the particular work that I am engaged in. Except for my friends, I had nothing I could think of to regret whatever. Certainly, I should like to have told them the story. But then one does not carry folios of paper in running shorts which have no pockets, and all my writing gear had gone by the board with the komatik.

I could still see a testimonial to myself some distance away in my khaki overalls, which I had left on another pan in the struggle of the night before. They seemed a kind of company, and would possibly be picked up and suggest the true story. Run-

ning through my head all the time,
quite unbidden, were the words of
the old hymn:

> "My God, my Father, while I stray
> Far from my home on life's dark way,
> Oh, teach me from my heart to say,
> Thy will be done!"

It is a hymn we hardly ever sing
out here, and it was an unconscious
memory of my boyhood days.

It was a perfect morning — a co-
balt sky, an ultramarine sea, a golden
sun, an almost wasteful extravagance
of crimson over hills of purest snow,
which caught a reflected glow from
rock and crag. Between me and the
hills lay miles of rough ice and long
veins of thin black slob that had
formed during the night. For the
foreground there was my poor, grue-
some pan, bobbing up and down on

the edge of the open sea, stained with blood, and littered with carcasses and débris. It was smaller than last night, and I noticed also that the new ice from the water melted under the dogs' bodies had been formed at the expense of its thickness. Five dogs, myself in colored football costume, and a bloody dogskin cloak, with a gay flannel shirt on a pole of frozen dogs' legs, completed the picture. The sun was almost hot by now, and I was conscious of a surplus of heat in my skin coat. I began to look longingly at one of my remaining dogs, for an appetite will rise even on an ice-pan, and that made me think of fire. So once again I inspected my matches. Alas! the heads were in paste, all but three or four blue-top wax ones.

These I now laid out to dry, while I searched about on my snow-pan to see if I could get a piece of transparent ice to make a burning-glass. For I was pretty sure that with all the unravelled tow I had stuffed into my leggings, and with the fat of my dogs, I could make smoke enough to be seen if only I could get a light. I had found a piece which I thought would do, and had gone back to wave my flag, which I did every two minutes, when I suddenly thought I saw again the glitter of an oar. It did not seem possible, however, for it must be remembered it was not water which lay between me and the land, but slob ice, which a mile or two inside me was very heavy. Even if people had seen me, I did not think they could get through, though I knew that the whole shore would then be trying. Moreover, there was no smoke rising on the land to give me hope that I had been seen. There had been no gun-flashes in the night, and I felt sure that, had any one seen me, there would have been a bonfire on every hill to encourage me to keep going.

So I gave it up, and went on with my work. But the next time I went back to my flag, the glitter seemed very distinct, and though it kept disappearing as it rose and fell on the surface, I kept my eyes strained upon it, for my dark spectacles had been lost, and I was partly snowblind.

I waved my flag as high as I could raise it, broadside on. At last, beside the glint of the white oar, I made out the black streak of the hull. I knew that, if the pan held on for another hour, I should be all right.

With that strange perversity of the human intellect, the first thing I thought of was what trophies I could carry with my luggage from the pan, and I pictured the dog-bone flagstaff adorning my study. (The dogs actually ate it afterwards.) I thought of preserving my ragged puttees with our collection of curiosities. I lost no time now at the burning-glass. My whole mind was devoted to making sure I should be seen, and I moved about as much as I dared on the raft, waving my sorry token aloft.

At last there could be no doubt about it: the boat was getting nearer and nearer. I could see that my rescuers were frantically waving, and,

when they came within shouting distance, I heard some one cry out,
"Don't get excited. Keep on the pan
where you are." They were infinitely
more excited than I. Already to me
it seemed just as natural now to be
saved as, half an hour before, it had
seemed inevitable I should be lost,
and had my rescuers only known, as
I did, the sensation of a bath in that
ice when you could not dry yourself
afterwards, they need not have expected me to follow the example of
the apostle Peter and throw myself
into the water.

As the man in the bow leaped
from the boat on to my ice raft and
grasped both my hands in his, not a
word was uttered. I could see in his
face the strong emotions he was trying hard to force back, though in

spite of himself tears trickled down his cheeks. It was the same with each of the others of my rescuers, nor was there any reason to be ashamed of them. These were not the emblems of weak sentimentality, but the evidences of the realization of the deepest and noblest emotion of which the human heart is capable, the vision that God has use for us his creatures, the sense of that supreme joy of the Christ — the joy of unselfish service. After the hand-shake and swallowing a cup of warm tea that had been thoughtfully packed in a bottle, we hoisted in my remaining dogs and started for home. To drive the boat home there were not only five Newfoundland fishermen at the oars, but five men with Newfoundland muscles in their backs, and five as brave hearts as ever beat in the bodies of human beings.

So, slowly but steadily, we forged through to the shore, now jumping out on to larger pans and forcing them apart with the oars, now hauling the boat out and dragging her over, when the jam of ice packed tightly in by the rising wind was impossible to get through otherwise.

My first question, when at last we found our tongues, was, ''How ever did you happen to be out in the boat in this ice?'' To my astonishment they told me that the previous night four men had been away on a long headland cutting out some dead harp seals that they had killed in the fall and left to freeze up in a rough wooden store they had built there, and that as they were leaving for home, my pan of ice had drifted out clear of Hare Island, and one of them, with his keen fisherman's eyes, had seen something unusual. They at once returned to their village, saying there was something alive drifting out to sea on the floe ice. But their report had been discredited, for the people thought that it could be only the top of some tree.

All the time I had been driving along I knew that there was one man on that coast who had a good spyglass. He tells me he instantly got up in the midst of his supper, on hearing the news, and hurried over the cliffs to the lookout, carrying his trusty spy-glass with him. Immediately, dark as it was, he saw that without any doubt there was a man out on the ice. Indeed, he saw me wave my hands every now and again towards the shore. By a very easy process of reasoning on so uninhabited a shore, he at once knew who it was, though some of the men argued that it must be some one else. Little had I thought, as night was closing in, that away on that snowy hilltop lay a man with a telescope patiently searching those miles of ice for *me*. Hastily they rushed back to the village and at once went down to try to launch a boat, but that proved to be impossible. Miles of ice lay between them and me, the heavy sea was hurling great blocks on the landwash, and night was already falling, the wind blowing hard on shore.

The whole village was aroused, and messengers were despatched at once along the coast, and lookouts told off to all the favorable points, so that while I considered myself a laughing-stock, bowing with my flag to those unresponsive cliffs, there were really many eyes watching me. One man told me that with his glass he distinctly saw me waving the shirt flag. There was little slumber that night in the villages, and even the men told me there were few dry eyes, as they thought of the impossibility of saving me from perishing. We are not given to weeping overmuch on this shore, but there are tears that do a man honor.

Before daybreak this fine volunteer crew had been gotten together. The boat, with such a force behind it of will power, would, I believe, have gone through anything. And, after seeing the heavy breakers

through which we were guided, loaded with their heavy ice battering-rams, when at last we ran through the harbor-mouth with the boat on our return, I knew well what wives and children had been thinking of when they saw their loved ones put out. Only two years ago I remember a fisherman's wife watching her husband and three sons take out a boat to bring in a stranger that was showing flags for a pilot. But the boat and its occupants have not yet come back.

Every soul in the village was on the beach as we neared the shore. Every soul was waiting to shake hands when I landed. Even with the grip that one after another gave me, some no longer trying to keep back the tears, I did not find out my hands were frost-burnt — a fact I have not been slow to appreciate since, however. I must have been a weird sight as I stepped ashore, tied up in rags, stuffed out with oakum, wrapped in the bloody skins of dogs, with no hat, coat, or gloves besides, and only a pair of short knickers. It must have seemed to some as if it were the old man of the sea coming ashore.

But no time was wasted before a pot of tea was exactly where I wanted it to be, and some hot stew was locating itself where I had intended an hour before the blood of one of my remaining dogs should have gone.

Rigged out in the warm garments that fishermen wear, I started with a large team as hard as I could race for the hospital, for I had learnt that the news had gone over that I was lost. It was soon painfully impressed upon me that I could not much enjoy the ride, for I had to be hauled like a log up the hills, my feet being frost-burnt so that I could not walk. Had I guessed this before going into the house, I might have avoided much trouble.

It is time to bring this egotistic narrative to an end. "Jack" lies curled up by my feet while I write this short account. "Brin" is once again leading and lording it over his fellows. "Doc" and the other survivors are not forgotten, now that we have again returned to the less romantic episodes of a mission hospital life. There stands in our hallway a bronze tablet to the memory of three noble dogs, Moody, Watch, and Spy, whose lives were given for mine on the ice.

In my home in England my brother has placed a duplicate tablet, and has added these words, ''Not one of them is forgotten before your Father which is in heaven.'' And this I most fully believe to be true. The boy whose life I was intent on saving was brought to the hospital a day or two later in a boat, the ice having cleared off the coast not to return for that season. He was operated on successfully, and is even now on the high road to recovery. We all love life. I was glad to be back once more with possibly a new lease of it before me. I had learned on the pan many things, but chiefly that the one cause for regret, when we look back on a life which we think is closed forever, will be the fact that we have wasted its opportunities. As I went to sleep that first night there still rang in my ea.'s the same verse of the old hymn which had been my companion on the ice, "Thy will, not mine, O Lord."

THE END

APPENDIX

APPENDIX

Oɴᴇ of Dr. Grenfell's volunteer helpers, Miss Luther of Providence, Rhode Island, contributes the following account of the rescue as recited in the Newfoundland vernacular by one of the rescuing party.

"One day, about a week after Dr. Grenfell's return," says Miss Luther, "two men came in from Griquet, fifteen miles away. They had walked all that distance, though the trail was heavy with soft snow and they often sank to their waists and waded through brooks and ponds. 'We just felt we must see the doctor and tell him what 'twould 'a' meant to us, if he'd been lost.' Perhaps nothing but the doctor's own tale could be more graphic than what was told by George Andrews, one of the crew who rescued him."

THE RESCUERS' STORY

"It was wonderfu' bad weather that Monday mornin'. Th' doctor was to Lock's Cove. None o' we thought o' 'is startin' out. I don't think th' doctor hisself thought o' going at first an' then 'e sent th' two men on ahead for to meet us at th' tilt an' said like's 'e was goin' after all.

"'Twas even' when us knew 'e was on th' ice. George Davis seen un first. 'E went to th' cliff to look for seal. It was after sunset an' half dark, but 'e thought 'e saw somethin' on th' ice an' 'e ran for George Read an' 'e got 'is spy-glass an' made out a man an' dogs on a pan an' knowed it war th' doctor.

"It was too dark fur we t' go t' un, but us never slept at all, all night. I couldn' sleep. Us watched th' wind an' knew if it didn' blow too hard us could get un — though 'e was then three mile off a'ready. So us waited for th' daylight. No one said who was goin' out in th' boat. Un 'ud say, 'Is you goin'?' An' another, 'Is you?' I didn' say, but I knowed what I'd do.

"As soon as 'twas light us went to th' cliff wi' th' spy-glass to see if us could see un, but thar warn't nothin' in sight. Us know by the wind whar t' look fur un, an' us launched th' boat. George Read an' 'is two sons, an' George Davis, what seen un first, an' me, was th' crew. George

[63]

Read was skipper-man an' th' rest was just youngsters. The sun was warm — you mind 'twas a fine mornin' — an' us started in our shirt an' braces, fur us knowed thar'd be hard work to do. I knowed thar was a chance o' not comin' back at all, but it didn' make no difference. I knowed I'd as good a chance as any, *an' 'twa' for th' doctor, an' 'is life's worth many*, an' somehow I couldn' let a man go out like dat wi'out tryin' fur un, an' I think us all felt th' same.

"Us 'ad a good strong boat an' four oars, an' took a hot kettle o' tea an' food for a week, for us thought u'd 'ave t' go far an' p'rhaps lose th' boat an' 'ave t' walk ashore un th' ice. I din' 'ope to find the doctor alive an' kept lookin' for a sign of un on th'

pans. 'Twa' no' easy gettin' to th'
pans wi' a big sea runnin'! Th' big
pans 'ud sometimes heave together
an' near crush th' boat, an' sometimes us 'ad t' git out an' haul her
over th' ice t' th' water again. Then
us come t' th' slob ice where th' pan
'ad ground together, an' 'twas all
thick, an' that was worse'n any. Us
saw th' doctor about twenty minutes
afore us got t' un. 'E was wavin' 'is
flag an' I seen 'im. 'E was on a pan
no bigger 'n this flor, an' I dunno
what ever kep' un fro' goin' abroad,
for 'twasn't ice, 'twas packed snow.
Th' pan was away from even th' slob,
floatin' by hisself, an' th' open water
all roun', an' 'twas just across fro'
Goose Cove, an' outside o' that there'd
been no hope. I think th' way th' pan
held together was on account o' th'

dogs' bodies meltin' it an' 't froze hard durin' th' night. 'E was level with th' water an' th' sea washin' over *us* all th' time.

"When us got near un, it didn' seem like 'twas th' doctor. 'E looked so old an' 'is face such a queer color. 'E was very solemn-like when us took un an' th' dogs on th' boat. No un felt like sayin' much, an' 'e 'ardly said nothin' till us gave un some tea an' loaf an' then 'e talked. I s'pose 'e was sort o' faint-like. Th' first thing 'e said was, how wonderfu' sorry 'e was o' gettin' into such a mess an' givin' we th' trouble o' comin' out for un. Us tol' un not to think o' that; us was glad to do it for un, an' 'e 'd done it for any one o' we, many times over if 'e 'ad th' chance; —an' so 'e would. An' then 'e fretted about th' b'y 'e was goin' to see, it bein' too late to reach un, an' us tol' un 'is life was worth so much more'n th' b'y, fur 'e could save others an' th' b'y couldn'. But 'e still fretted.

"'E 'ad ripped th' dog-harnesses an' stuffed th' oakum in th' legs o' 'is pants to keep un warm. 'E showed it to we. An' 'e cut off th' tops o' 'is boots to keep th' draught from 'is back. 'E must 'a' worked 'ard all night. 'E said 'e droled off once or twice, but th' night seemed wonderfu' long.

"Us took un off th' pan at about half-past seven, an' 'ad a 'ard fight gettin' in, th' sea still runnin' 'igh. 'E said 'e was proud to see us comin' for un, and so 'e might, for it grew wonderfu' cold in th' day and th' sea so 'igh the pan couldn' 'a' lived outside. 'E wouldn' stop when us got ashore, but must go right on, an' when 'e 'ad dry clothes an' was a bit warm, us sent un to St. Anthony with a team.

"Th' next night, an' for nights after, I couldn' sleep. I'd keep seein' that man standin' on th' ice, an I'd be sorter half-awake like, sayin', 'But not th' doctor. Sure *not* th' *doctor*.'"

There was silence for a few moments, and George Andrews looked out across the blue harbor to the sea.

"'E sent us watches an' spy-glasses," said he, "an' pictures o' hisself that one o' you took o' un, made large an' in a frame. George Read an' me 'ad th' watches an' th' others 'ad th' spy-glasses. 'Ere 's th' watch. It 'as 'In memory o' April 21st' on it, but us don't need th' things to make we remember it, tho' we 're wonderful glad t' 'ave 'em from th' doctor."

TO THE MEMORY OF
THREE NOBLE DOGS

MOODY.

WATCH.

SPY.

WHOSE LIVES WERE GIVEN
FOR MINE ON THE ICE.
April 21st 1908.
WILFRED GRENFELL,
ST. ANTHONY.

MEMORIAL TABLET AT ST. ANTHONY'S
HOSPITAL NEWFOUNDLAND.

DATE DUE.

Feb 6			
Feb 21			
Mar 9			